DISCARD

BEETLE

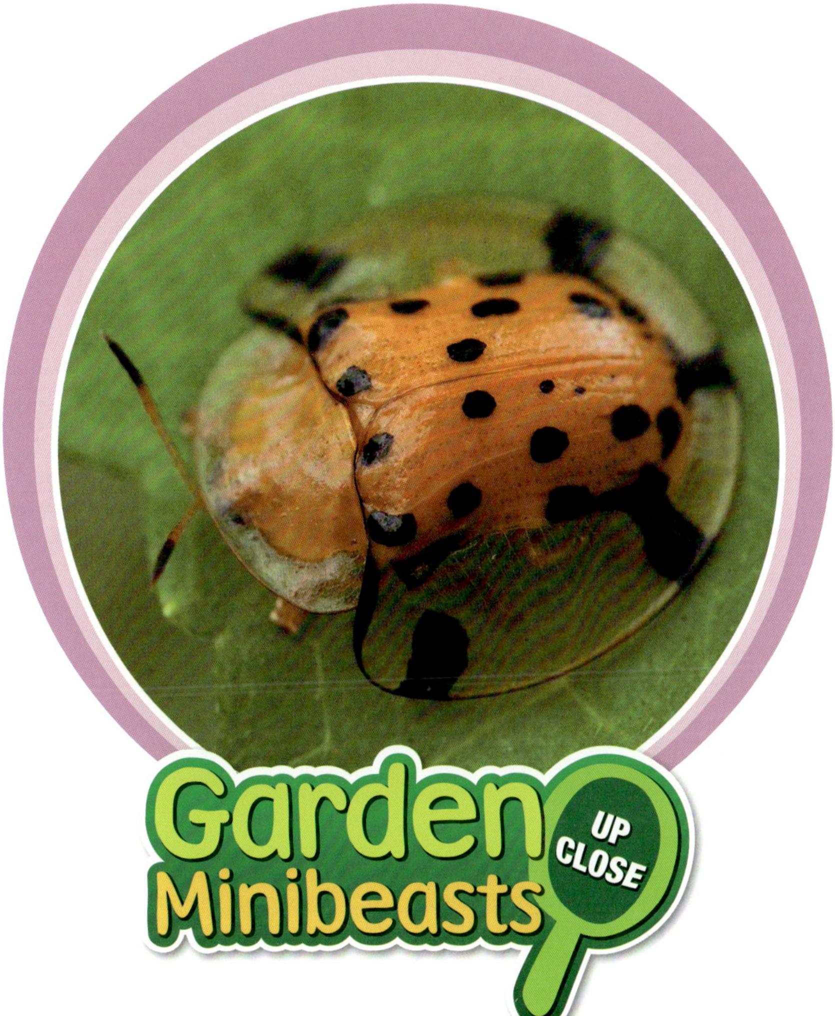

Garden Minibeasts UP CLOSE

John Woodward

An Imprint of Chelsea House Publishers

Beetle

© 2010 by Infobase Publishing

All rights reserved. No part of this book may be reproduced or utilized in any form or by any means, electronic or mechanical, including photocopying, recording, or by any information storage or retrieval systems, without permission in writing from the publisher. For information contact:

Chelsea Clubhouse
An imprint of Chelsea House
132 West 31st Street
New York, NY 10001

Library of Congress Cataloging-in-Publication Data
Woodward, John, 1954-
  Beetle / John Woodward.
    p. cm. -- (Garden minibeasts up close)
  Includes bibliographical references and index.
  ISBN 978-1-60413-897-9
  1. Beetles--Juvenile literature. I. Title. II. Series: Woodward, John, 1954- Garden minibeasts up close.
  QL576.2.W66 2010
  595.76--dc22
                    2009052776

Chelsea Clubhouse books are available at special discounts when purchased in bulk quantities for businesses, associations, institutions, or sales promotions. Please call our Special Sales Department in New York at (212) 967-8800 or (800) 322-8755.

You can find Chelsea Clubhouse on the World Wide Web at http://www.chelseahouse.com

Produced for Chelsea House by Discovery Books
Managing Editor: Laura Durman
Project Editor: Colleen Ruck
Picture Researcher: Colleen Ruck
Designer: Blink Media
Illustrator: Stuart Lafford

Photo acknowledgments: FLPA: pp 4 (Nigel Cattlin), 10 (Nigel Cattlin), 11 (Mark Moffett/Minden Pictures), 16 (Mark Moffett/Minden Pictures), 27 (Mark Moffett/Minden Pictures); Photolibrary: p 21 (Bill Beatty); Photoshot: pp 9 (John Brackenbury), 19 (John Shaw), 20 (Jeff Greenberg), 25 (Stephen Dalton); Terry Priest www.frfly.com: p 24; Shutterstock Images: pp 5 (Goran Cakmazovic), 7 (Liudmila Gridina), 8 (Juliya Shumskaya), 12 (Henrik Larsson), 13 (Marek R. Swadzba), 14 (Sharon Day), 15 (orionmystery@flickr), 17 (Joy Stein), 18 (Dirk Ercken), 23 (Argonaut), 26 (Kirsanov), 28 (image shutter).

Cover printed by Bang Printing, Brainerd, MN
Book printed and bound by Bang Printing, Brainerd, MN
Date printed April 2010
Printed in the United States of America

10 9 8 7 6 5 4 3 2 1

This book is printed on acid-free paper.

All links and Web addresses were checked and verified to be correct at the time of publication. Because of the dynamic nature of the Web, some addresses and links may have changed since publication and may no longer be valid.

Contents

🪲	Finding beetles	4
🪲	A beetle's body	6
🪲	Life cycles	8
🪲	Hungry young	10
🪲	Fierce hunters	12
🪲	Plant eaters	14
🪲	Dung and carrion beetles	16
🪲	Water beetles	18
🪲	Beetle defenses	20
🪲	Males and females	22
🪲	Fireflies and glow-worms	24
🪲	Beautiful beetles	26
🪲	Beetles and people	28
🪲	Glossary	30
🪲	Further resources	31
🪲	Index	32

Finding beetles

You won't have to look far to find a beetle. They live almost everywhere. Beetles are the most successful animals on the planet! Check any flowers near your home. Many beetles feed on flower **nectar** or **pollen**.

Did You Know?
Some beetles spend their lives inside buildings. Carpet beetles eat woolen carpets, while museum beetles even eat insects that are on display in museums!

Ladybugs like this one are probably the easiest beetles to find. Their bright colors warn birds that they taste awful.

The brightly colored ladybugs that hunt other insects on plants are beetles. Other beetles hunt over the ground for small animals and often hide beneath stones. Try turning over a rock or two. You might be surprised by what crawls out.

A beetle's body

When you look at a beetle, the first thing you notice is the hard shell covering its back. The shell is split into two parts called the **elytra**. When these open, you can see a pair of wings underneath. Beetles use the elytra as front wings when they fly, too.

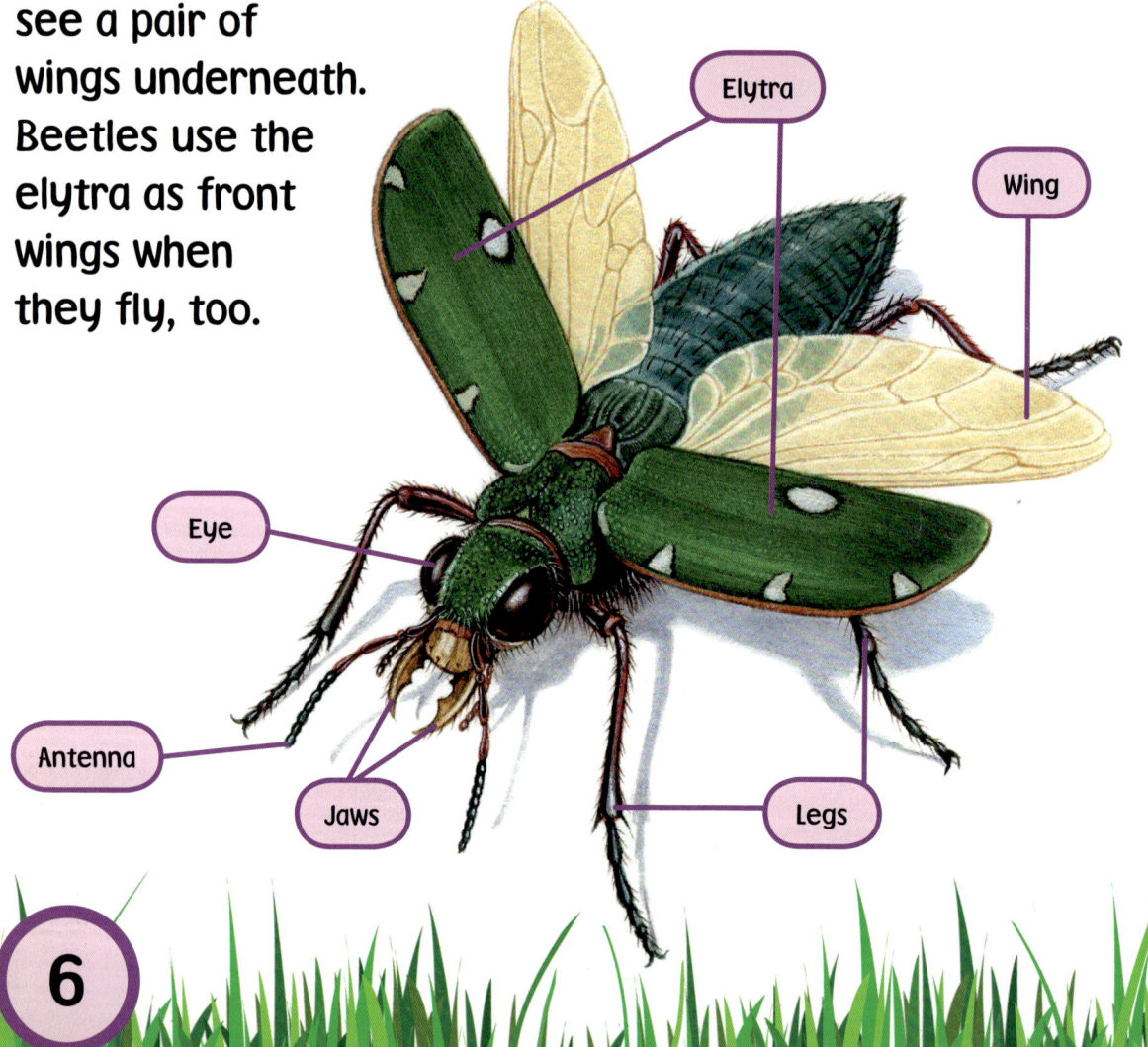

Get up close and you will see that a beetle's eyes are very big. All beetles also have feelers, or **antennae**. These pick up smells and can sense movement.

Did You Know?

You might call a beetle a bug, but a true bug is an insect with sucking mouthparts instead of biting jaws. Some bugs have hardened wing cases like beetles. On bugs, the tips cross over instead of meeting at the middle.

The bright elytra of this beautiful creature show that it is a beetle.

Life cycles

Have you ever found a white, wriggly insect **grub** in the bottom of a flowerpot? If so, it was probably a baby beetle such as a vine **weevil**.

A beetle's life cycle is in four stages. First the mother lays eggs that hatch into grubs, or **larvae**.

These eggs are attached to a potato leaf. They will hatch as leaf-eating Colorado beetle larvae.

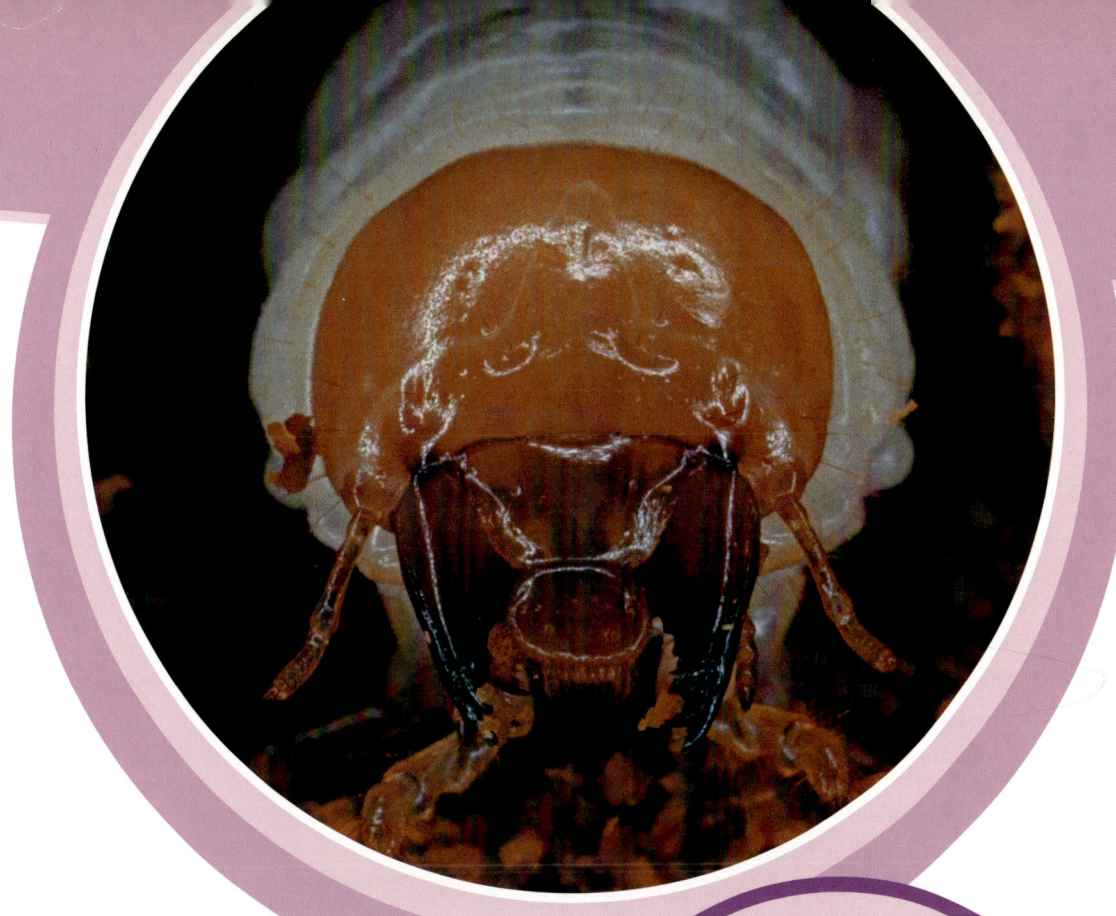

Larvae burrow through the soil and feed on plant roots. Often, they can harm or even kill the plant. Eventually the larvae become **pupae**, which, in turn, become adult beetles.

Did You Know?

Some beetles such as American stag beetles live for many years as burrowing larvae (shown above), but they only live for a few weeks as adults. The adults may not eat at all and survive just long enough to **breed**.

Hungry young

Did You Know?
Some ladybug larvae are **cannibals!** They will eat each other if they run short of other **prey** such as **aphids**.

A black bean aphid makes a tasty meal for this ladybug larva. Unlike most beetle larvae, it is an active hunter.

Young beetles are always hungry and eat nearly all the time. Many chew through plants, while some attack other insects. For example, a ladybug larva eats about 20 small plant bugs a day.

They eat so much because they are growing fast. Eventually they turn into adults and stop growing altogether. Adult beetles do not need to eat as much—and some don't eat at all!

The bess beetle larva eats rotting wood. This beetle is unusual because its parents (below) gather and chew its food for it.

Fierce hunters

You've probably seen beetles running over the ground, looking very busy. These are usually hunters that catch and eat other animals. They have big eyes for spotting their prey, and powerful biting jaws.

Did You Know?
The larvae of tiger beetles live in holes in the ground. Each larva sits in the bottom with its jaws open like a trap, ready to snap up any insects that fall in its hole.

With its big eyes and fearsome jaws, this tiger beetle is well equipped for attacking other insects.

The ground beetle is a common hunter in backyards.

In the backyard you are likely to come across dark, slim ground beetles. They prey on many different kinds of small animals, including bugs, worms, and even slimy slugs.

The fiercest beetles are the colorful, metallic tiger beetles. They are found in dry, sandy places.

Plant eaters

Do you like salad and vegetables? Plenty of beetles do, too. Leaf beetles chew through leaves, and chafer beetles and scarabs eat flowers and fruit. Flower beetles eat the powdery pollen from flowers or sip their sweet, sugary nectar.

Flower nectar and pollen provide this Pennsylvania leather-wing beetle with all the food it needs.

Did You Know?

Big diving beetles are hunters that attack other small animals. Their larvae are even more ferocious. They bite animals including fish and tadpoles with their long, curved, hollow **fangs**. Then they suck them dry.

Diving beetles need to breathe air, so they carry an air supply as a silvery bubble trapped under their elytra.

A diving beetle larva (brown) attacks a mosquito larva with its sharp fangs.

Beetle defenses

Do you want to pick up a big beetle? Be careful—some can bite! Beetles are very well **armored**, often with defensive **spines**. Some have sharp jaws, too.

Many have other defenses as well. The amazing bombardier beetle defends itself by spraying boiling chemicals from its rear end. It does this by mixing two fluids that explode on contact with each other!

It may look harmless, but the little bombardier beetle can give its enemies an explosive surprise!

The spots on this click beetle's head are designed to scare away enemies who mistake them for large eyes.

Some beetles taste bad or produce smelly fluids to try and stop other animals from eating them. These beetles are often brightly colored to warn enemies to stay away.

Did You Know?

A click beetle "plays dead" to trick its enemies. If this fails, it leaps to freedom by suddenly snapping its tail against the ground with a loud click.

Males and females

Trying to figure out whether a beetle is a male or female is often close to impossible. They usually look alike, but there can be a few clues. Male stag beetles have huge jaws. They use these to wrestle rivals in fights over females. The winner **mates** with the female, who then goes off to lay her eggs.

> Sometimes a fighting male stag beetle will lift his rival right off the ground and toss him onto his back.

Did You Know?

Although the huge jaws of male stag beetles look ferocious, their jaw muscles are not strong enough to bite you very hard. A bite from the shorter, sharper jaws of a female (shown here) can be much more painful!

Some male beetles have longer antennae. These detect the special **scent** released by females. In a few types of beetle, the males can fly but the females cannot.

Fireflies and glow-worms

Go out on a dark summer evening and you might see flashing lights in the trees. These aren't fairies, but fireflies, which are really small beetles. Male and female fireflies flash **coded** messages to each other from trees and bushes and from the air.

The big eyes of this male firefly help him spot the signals of flashing females.

Female glow-worms have no wings, and rely on the males to find them. It's not difficult, of course!

Did You Know?
Some fireflies are killers. They attract other types of fireflies by copying their flash-code—and then eat them when they land.

Similarly, female glow-worms sit in the grass and glow to attract flying males.

Beautiful beetles

Even an ordinary black dung beetle can glow with a rainbow of colors in bright sunlight.

You may not think of beetles as beautiful creatures, but some are really stunning. Their armored bodies glitter with a rainbow of colors and look like precious metals or gems.

You might find some of these wonderful creatures in your backyard. Many are very small, though, so you have to look hard!

Beetles that visit flowers are often very attractive. Some are rare because people collect them for their beauty.

Did You Know?
In India and some other eastern countries the elytra of beetles are used as jewelry. They can also be used to decorate clothes for special ceremonies.

The golden scarab beetle from Arizona is one of the most spectacular insects living in the United States.

Beetles and people

Some beetles can be real pests. The boll weevil is famous for destroying cotton crops. It costs U.S. farmers about $300 million a year!

Other beetle pests include the potato-eating Colorado beetle and the bark beetles that kill trees. Carpet beetle larvae can be a pest in homes, while wood-boring beetle larvae can turn timber to dust.

Colorado beetles can destroy whole crops of potatoes.

Weevils gnaw on seeds and nuts as well as roots. Amazingly, the larvae of bark beetles and stag beetles can chew through solid wood. They make long tunnels that get wider as the larvae grow. But wood is not a very good food, so many of these timber-borers grow very slowly over many years.

Did You Know?

Some beetle larvae live inside leaves. They burrow through them leaving long trails. They are called leaf miners and you can often find them in the backyard.

The long snout of this weevil is tipped with small, sharp jaws for breaking into nuts.

Dung and carrion beetles

How would you like a breakfast of cow **dung** or a dinner of dead mice? For some beetles they are a favorite food, and we should be thankful to them. They get rid of animal dung and dead creatures by using them as food for their young.

Did You Know?
Female **carrion** beetles are one of the few insects that care for their young. They guard them in their burrows and feed them with meat from the animals they bury.

A mother carrion beetle feeds her larvae.

This dung beetle is collecting a ball of animal dung. It will bury it as a food store for its young.

Some dung beetles roll dung into balls. They push the ball over the ground with their legs while walking backward. It's a neat trick! The female lays an egg in the middle of each ball. Then the male and female work together to bury it.

Water beetles

You may find a beetle or two living in your local pond or lake. The most obvious are the little whirligig beetles. They live in groups on the surface of the water. They are named for the way they whirl around in circles.

Other beetles dive underwater to find food. Their legs have feathery fringes. They use these to push themselves along.

Big diving beetles chase and eat other animals. They push themselves through the water with their oar-like legs.

Did You Know?

In the town of Enterprise, Alabama, there is a monument to the boll weevil (shown right). It was put up in 1919 after the insect destroyed the local cotton industry. This forced farmers to grow other crops such as peanuts that actually made them more money!

Some beetles, such as ladybugs, help us by eating other plant pests. And most beetles do not affect us at all.

Glossary

antennae: The "feelers" on the head of a beetle. It uses them to feel its way around and to pick up scents.

aphids: Small bugs such as greenfly that suck the sugary sap of plants.

armored: Having a tough outer covering that protects the body.

breed: To multiply by producing young.

cannibal: An animal that eats other animals of the same species.

carrion: Meat from dead animals.

code: A secret language that is only understood by those who know how it works.

dung: Animal poop, or excrement.

elytra: The scientific word for beetle wing cases.

fangs: Special teeth that are hollow and used to inject poison.

grub: The soft-bodied young stage, or larva, of a beetle.

larva: The young life stage of an insect, when it does most of its feeding. A beetle grub is a larva. Plural is larvae.

mate: When males and females come together to produce young.

nectar: The scented, sugary fluid produced by flowers to attract animals such as insects.

pollen: Tiny grains produced by flowers.

prey: An animal that is attacked and eaten by another animal.

pupa: The life stage of an insect when it changes from the young form (larva) to an adult. Plural is pupae.

scent: A strong smell

spines: Long, sharp points.

weevil: A type of beetle with a long snout that feeds on plants.

Further resources

Books

Donovan, Sandy Bridget. *Beetles.* Chicago: Heinemann-Raintree, 2008.
Discover the exciting and colorful beetles that live in rain forests.

Hartley, Karen. *Beetles.* Chicago: Heinemann-Raintree, 2008.
An introduction to beetles, containing lots of interesting information.

Markle, Sandra. *Diving Beetles.* Minneapolis: Lerner Publications, 2008.
A close-up look at these exciting beetles.

Prischmann, Deirdre A. *Poop-Eaters: Dung Beetles in the Food Chain.* Mankato: Capstone Press, 2008.
Find out about the dung beetle's place in the food chain and how it helps the environment.

Twist, Clint. *Dung Beetles.* Strongsville/New York: Gareth Stevens Publishing, 2006.
This book explores the amazing world of dung beetles.

Walker, Sally. *Fireflies.* Minneapolis: Lerner Publications, 2001.
Learn all about these fascinating creatures, and their ability to produce light.

Web sites

Cirrus Image, "Beetles" *http://www.cirrusimage.com/beetle.htm*
When you find a beetle in your backyard, use the photographs on this Web site to figure out what type of beetle it is.

National Geographic, "Creature Feature: Dung Beetles"
http://kids.nationalgeographic.com/Animals/CreatureFeature/Dung-beetle
This Web site contains lots of facts and information about dung beetles. Watch a video of a dung beetle making a ball of dung.

Pestworld For Kids, "Beetles" *http://www.pestworldforkids.org/beetles.html*
A look at some different types of beetle, where you might find them, their eating habits and how to keep them from becoming a pest.

The Beetle Experience, *http://www.beetle-experience.com/gallery-1l.htm*
A gallery of North American beetle images and information. This Web site also gives information about how to look after a beetle as a pet!

Index

antennae 7, 23

bark beetle 15, 28
bess beetle 11
big diving beetle 18-19
boll weevil 28, 29
bombardier beetle 20

carpet beetle 4, 28
carrion beetle 16
chafers 14
click beetle 21
Colorado beetle 8, 28

diving beetles 18-19
dung beetle 16-17, 26

eggs 8, 22
elytra 6, 7, 19, 27
eyes 6, 7, 12, 21, 24

firefly 24, 25
flower beetles 14
food 4, 9, 10-11, 12, 13 14-15, 16, 25, 29

glow-worm 25
golden scarab beetle 27
ground beetle 13
grubs *see* larvae

hunting 5, 10, 12-13, 19

jaws 6, 7, 12, 15, 20, 22, 23

ladybug 5, 10, 29
larvae 8, 9, 10, 12, 13, 15, 16, 19, 28
life cycles 8-9
    feeding 10-11, 16
    hunters 19
    pests 28
leaf beetles 14
leaf miners 15
life cycle 8-9

museum beetle 4

Pennsylvania leather-wing beetle 14
pests 28-29

scarabs 14. 27
stag beetle 9, 15, 22-23

tiger beetle 12, 13

vine weevil 8

water beetles 18-19
weevils 8, 15, 28
whirligig beetle 18
wings 6
wood-boring beetles 28